Henry Grier Bryant

A Journey To The Grand Falls Of Labrador

Henry Grier Bryant

A Journey To The Grand Falls Of Labrador

ISBN/EAN: 9783741118081

Manufactured in Europe, USA, Canada, Australia, Japa

Cover: Foto ©Andreas Hilbeck / pixelio.de

Manufactured and distributed by brebook publishing software
(www.brebook.com)

Henry Grier Bryant

A Journey To The Grand Falls Of Labrador

A JOURNEY TO

THE GRAND FALLS OF LABRADOR*

BY

HENRY G. BRYANT, M.A., LL.B.

Recording Secretary Geographical Club of Philadelphia.

It is a suggestive fact that the great peninsula of Labrador, although probably the first part of the American
mainland to be seen by Europeans, contains to-day the
largest unexplored area on the Western Continent. Without disputing the evidence of the Norse records, which
ascribe to the Vikings priority in discovering America ; and,
whether or not, we admit that the landfall of John Cabot
in 1497 was Labrador, as maintained by many, or a more
southerly point on the coast, it seems certain from con-
temporary chronicles, that Sebastian Cabot, on his second
voyage, cruised along the coast of Labrador as early as

* A preliminary account of the Grand Falls of Labrador appeared in *The
Century Magazine*, for September, 1892. The greater part of that article is
embodied in the present paper, and, for permission to reprint, with the
accompanying illustrations, the author acknowledges his indebtedness to
The Century Company.

I

July, 1498; whereas Columbus did not reach the mainland of South America, near the mouth of the Orinoco River, until August 1st of the same year.[1]

Following in the wake of the Cortereals, Jacques Cartier and other explorers, these Northern shores became the resort of Basque, Breton and English fishermen, who here reaped the rich harvest of the sea and left behind memorials of their presence, in the shape of scattered ruins and a string of geographical names which possess an old-world character which is unmistakable.

In later times, the Labrador coast has continued to be the rendezvous of a large fleet of fishermen, whose numbers are recruited, in the main, from the neighboring colony of Newfoundland; these hardy seamen possess an intimate knowledge of the coast; but their interests being wholly connected with the sea, the interior has remained a mystery to them, while to their agency, more than any other, must be ascribed the reputation which has gone abroad of the Arctic climate and desolate interior of Labrador. It is undoubtedly true that the 760 miles of rocky seaboard stretching from the Strait of Belle Isle to Cape Chudleigh well merits the reputation given it by all travellers, as a savage and sterile coast unique in its wild desolation. The climate, likewise, is most severe as a result of the ice-laden

---

[1] For a critical discussion of early voyages to Labrador, as well as a comprehensive account of the geography, geology and inhabitants of the coast, *vide :* Prof. A. H. Packard's recent work, *The Labrador Coast.* New York, 1891.

Referring to the voyages of the Cabots, the author quotes (p. 36) the German author Johann Georg Kohl: "'Although on their return from their first voyage of 1497 the Cabots believed that the land they had discovered was some part of Asia, to them must be given the credit of beholding the American continent before Columbus; while, with little or no doubt, Sebastian Cabot beheld in July, 1498, the mainland of Labrador, for, says Hakluyt, "Columbus first saw the firme lande, August 1, 1498." '"

Arctic current which passes along the coast. This current, with the north-east polar winds, produces a mean annual temperature, which at many places is below the freezing point. But the interior presents conditions much more attractive, and having advanced inland a short distance from the coast, a marked improvement is apparent. The forbidding character of the coast, however, has given a false impression of the whole country, and in this we must find explanation of the fact that Labrador has so rarely been visited by travellers, while many less accessible parts of the earth have gradually yielded up their secrets.

From the time of the early navigators to the present, various maps embracing the Labrador peninsula have been published. An examination of these reveals most strikingly the absence of accurate information, more especially in relation to the interior. Of the great rivers—the natural highways to the interior—the ignorance of geographers has been commensurate with their information relating to other physical features of the country, and none of the maps portray the fluvial systems and great inland lakes with any degree of precision. The existence of a great table-land in the interior has long been known. This elevated plateau extends to the coast in the northeastern part of the peninsula, and here it is said to attain a great height, rising precipitously from the sea and supporting mountains, some of which reach an altitude of six thousand feet.[2] At a point north of Hamilton Inlet the line of this platform seems to recede from the coast trending in a south-easterly direction towards the Gulf of St. Lawrence. The interior portion of the plateau probably attains its greatest elevation at a point somewhat south of

[2] Dr. Robert Bell. *Report Geological and Natural History Survey of Canada. 1885. Vol. I, p. 8, D.D.*

the geographical centre of this elevated region. Here the
great rivers of the peninsula have their source; and here
the central water-shed of the country is located where,
within a comparatively limited area, elevated, lacustrine
basins discharge their waters north into Ungava Bay, east
into the Atlantic Ocean, south into the Gulf of St. Lawrence and west into Hudson Bay.[3]

The most important stream which flows towards the
Atlantic seaboard is the Grand, or Hamilton River, which
rises in the lakes on this upland and flows in a general
south-easterly direction into Hamilton Inlet—the great arm
of the sea which, under various names, penetrates the
interior a distance of one hundred and fifty miles. No scientific explorer has advanced far into the country, and the
imperfect knowledge of the interior rests almost entirely
on the vague reports of Indians, a few missionaries, and
information furnished by agents of the Hudson's Bay Company. In fact, of the interior of this vast territory, estimated to contain two hundred and eighty-nine thousand
square miles,[4] but little is known; notwithstanding it is
much nearer England and the United States than many
portions of the globe which are frequently visited by
travellers and scientists.

A variety of considerations have combined to bring
about this condition of affairs: the reputation for sterility
which has attached itself to the country, the brevity of
the summer season, the difficulty of navigating the rivers,

---

[3] While at North-west River Post, in September, 1891, I was informed
by two aged *voyageurs* of the Hudson's Bay Company, who had made frequent journeys to the "Height of Land," that this water-shed is found not
far from the site of Fort Nascopie, an outpost long since abandoned by the
Company.

[4] Dr. G. M. Dawson. Paper read before the Field Naturalists' Club of
Ottawa, 1890.

the absence of any commercial incentive and the indifference or inability of the governments concerned, all have
united to bring about the present condition of unenlighten-
ment. Labrador, consequently, has presented a comparatively new field to the explorer. It will be of interest to
note briefly such geographical researches as have been
undertaken from time to time.

As is well known, missions of the Moravian Church
have been established on the coast for over a hundred
years, the earliest one, Nain, dating from 1770. In 1811,
the brethren of one of the northern establishments
explored the coast of Ungava Bay, which had previously
been entered by Weymouth as far back as 1602. The missionaries subsequently published a pamphlet, describing
the Ungava district as a comparatively fertile area and as
offering a suitable field for missionary effort among the
heathen Eskimos of the north coast. According to Mr.
W. H. A. Davies, who published a description of the
Ungava neighborhood,[5] the appearance of this pamphlet
first called the attention of the Hudson's Bay Company to
this part of Labrador, with the result that Fort Chimo was
built on the Koksoak River, twenty-seven miles distant from
Ungava Bay, in 1827. Referring to the attempts of the
Company to investigate the interior, Davies says : " . . .
it was not until 1834 that any efforts were made to explore
the interior to the southward and eastward. In that year,
a clerk of the Company left Fort Chimo on the sixth of
April, to explore the country to Mingan, but when on the
height of land, his guide refused to conduct him there,
and brought him to Esquimaux Bay, where he arrived on
the twenty-second of June, being the first European who had

---

[5] W. H. A. Davies. *Notes on Ungava Bay and its Vicinity. Transac-
tions Literary and Historical Society of Quebec. 1854.*

traversed the interior in that direction." Davies obtained
his data from Mr. John M'Lean, who was the company's
agent at Fort Chimo from 1837 to 1842. In the year 1839,
this officer, while seeking to find a more practical route
than the one heretofore used between Ungava Bay and
Esquimaux Bay, traversed the northern part of the peninsula in canoes, travelling from north to south. He reached
the most inland outpost of the Company, Fort Nascopie,
which had recently been established on Lake Petchikapou.
Finding a large stream, which he subsequently identified
as the Grand River, issuing from the lake, he boldly set
out to navigate it, hoping it would lead in the desired
direction. While moving down this river, where no white
man had been before, M'Lean discovered the Grand Falls
of Labrador, which proved a barrier to his further descent
of the river. Being thus frustrated in his design to estab-
lish an inland route to North-west River Post, and finding
the river for many miles below the Falls inaccessible, he
abandoned his project, and says: "With heavy hearts and
weary limbs we retraced our steps." M'Lean, however,
subsequently learned from the Indians of a chain of lakes
by which the Falls and Caññon could be circumvented, and
this route was used by the Hudson's Bay Company for
many years in sending supplies from the head of Hamilton
Inlet (Esquimaux Bay) to Fort Nascopie, the inland post
before referred to.

After resigning from the Company and returning to
civilization, M'Lean published a graphic account of his
adventures in Labrador, and his brief description of the
Falls possesses great interest, as that of the first white
man who ever gazed on this remote cataract.[6] The tradi-

---

[6] John M'Lean. *Notes of a Twenty-five Years' Service in the Hudson's Bay Territory.* London, 1849.

tions of the Hudson's Bay Company affirm that twenty
years after M'Lean's visit, the Grand Falls were again
visited by an officer of the company, Joseph McPherson,
who while on his way to Fort Nascopie, made a detour
from the established route for the purpose of examining
the Falls. He was guided to the spot by an Iroquois
Indian named Louis-over-the-fire, who lived until Novem-
ber, 1892, an aged pensioner of the Company, at North-west
River Post. These are the only white men who, previous
to the summer of 1891, are known to have seen the Grand
Falls.[7]   Neither M'Lean nor McPherson measured the
height of the Falls, and, in fact, it does not appear that
the latter ever gave any account of his visit to this region.
To continue the brief record of Labrador exploration,
mention should be made of the journey of Prof. H. Y.
Hind, who thirty-two years ago started from the Seven
Islands, on the St. Lawrence coast, and ascended the Moisie
River, a distance of one hundred and twenty miles.
Strictly speaking, the territory drained by this affluent of
the St. Lawrence is not in Labrador proper, but is em-
braced within the eastern borders of the province of
Quebec.

In the account of his explorations, Prof. Hind
gives the height of the interior plateau of Labrador as
something over two thousand two hundred feet, and this

---

[7] Subsequent to my departure for Labrador, I learned of another
American expedition, under the auspices of Bowdoin College, which pro-
posed to visit the Labrador coast during the summer of 1891. The plans
of this expedition included the despatching up the Grand River of a sub-
sidiary party of four students. The inland party entered the mouth of the
river on July 27th, and two members of it, Messrs. Austin Cary and D. M.
Cole, succeeded in reaching the Falls on August 13, 1891. Mr. Cary published an account of his journey in *Bulletin American Geographical Society*,
Vol. XXIV, p. 1.

idea has been accepted by most writers on the subject.[8]
Now ensued a long period, during which no traveller or
trader disturbed the loneliness of this remote wilderness.
Fort Nascopie, the interior post of the Hudson's Bay
Company, was abandoned some twenty-nine years ago, and
the Indian trail which led to it and passed within fifty
miles of the Falls was disused in the interval. No one
endeavored to ascend the Grand River, and the dim tradition of the Falls was almost forgotten.

At length, in 1887, an English traveller, Mr. R. F.
Holme, of Oxford University, journeyed to Labrador and
started up the Grand River, having the Falls as the objec-
tive point of his expedition. He relied on Prof. Hind's
statement that the cataract was a hundred miles from
the mouth of the river, and consequently found himself
insufficiently equipped for what proved to be a much
longer journey. With a boat and two men he pluckily
surmounted the difficulties of river navigation, and
reached a point about a hundred and forty miles from the
mouth of the river, when he was obliged to turn back by
the failure of his provisions. Mr. Holme read an account
of his journey before the Royal Geographical Society,
and I am indebted to this narrative for much valuable
information regarding the river and the conditions pre-
vailing in the country.[9]

I am informed that another attempt to reach the Falls
was made in the summer of 1890, by Mr. J. G. Alwyn
Creighton, of Ottawa, Canada, who sailed down the Gulf
of St. Lawrence as far as the mouth of the St. Augustine
River, where he secured canoes and Indian guides and

[8] H. Y. Hind. *The Labrador Peninsula. Vol. II, p. 134.* London,
1863.
[9] *Proceedings Royal Geographical Society. April, 1888.*

ascended the river a considerable distance, hoping to reach the waters of the Grand River by an overland route much used by the natives. Unfortunately, he encountered one of those great forest fires which seem to periodically desolate great areas in Labrador. After losing some time in attempting, without success, to overcome this obstacle, he was compelled by the want of provisions to relinquish his project and return home.

My attention was first drawn to the Grand Falls of Labrador in the early spring of 1891, by reading a fugitive newspaper article on the subject. The writer referred to the stories current among the Indians and *voyageurs*, which tended to prove the existence of a great waterfall in the interior. The author seemed inclined to accept the legendary accounts of the cataract, which ascribed to it the stupendous height of one thousand five hundred feet. There was something in the very idea of this distant cataract—thundering on for ages in that far-off land—which appealed forcibly to one's imagination and seemed to mark the spot as a worthy goal for some traveller willing to penetrate the interior and verify the reports long current as to the height and location of this natural wonder. After further investigation, the conviction was strengthened that a visit to the Grand Falls presented no insurmountable obstacles. Confident, therefore, that such a trip would yield interesting geographical results and exciting sport with rod and gun, I determined to essay the voyage.

I was fortunate in obtaining in Prof. C. A. Kenaston, of Washington, D. C., an associate who entered with enthusiasm into my plans. Preparations for the journey were made in the early part of June, 1891. The various articles of equipment were gotten together with some care, and included, among other things, a Rushton canoe sixteen feet in length.

We sailed from New York June 23d, on the steamship *Portia,* and arrived at St. Johns, Newfoundland, on the twenty-ninth of the same month. After an unexpected and vexatious delay here of over two weeks, we sailed from St. Johns on July 15th, on the small steamship *Curlew,* the boat engaged by the Newfoundland Government to carry the mails on the Labrador coast during the summer. After calling at several ports on the north-eastern coast of Newfoundland, our stanch little craft turned north, and, steaming through the dense fogs of the Strait of Belle Isle, we soon caught our first glimpse of the Labrador coast. The four days' sail along this coast was the most enjoyable part of the voyage. Space will not permit me to make any extended reference to the novelty and grandeur of the scenery which formed so impressive an introduction to this rugged north-land which was to be the scene of our wanderings. The shores presented a bold, irregular line of hills, wild and desolate in their aspect, and for the most part entirely destitute of verdure ; their precipitous bases presenting bold headlands to the waves of the Atlantic. Icebergs soon became frequent.   In one day I counted twenty-six.   Our fellow-passengers, most of whom were engaged in the fisheries, viewed these Polar visitors with the indifference born of familiarity; but for my part, I regarded these majestic, luminous white masses with the keenest interest.

On July 23d, we arrived at Rigolet, in Hamilton Inlet. This is the chief station of the Hudson's Bay Company in Labrador, and at the time of our visit, Chief Factor P. W. Bell, a veteran officer of the Company, was in charge of the post.   We were provided with letters of introduction

and were most hospitably received. A small schooner
being placed at our disposal, the following day we continued our journey into the interior, sailing westward
through the great interior basin known as Melville, or
Grosswater Bay. The Mealy Mountains stretch along
the southern shore almost the entire length of the bay.
Although it was midsummer, patches of snow were conspicuous on their northern slopes. At the entrance to
Hamilton Inlet, the distant peaks of this range are seen
stretching away to the south. Southwest of the contracted
channel called " The Narrows," on which Rigolet is situ-
ated, the Mealy Mountains approach Melville Bay, giving
a picturesque aspect to the southern shore of that great
salt water basin. These mountains rise quite abruptly a
few miles from the bay and appear to have an average height
of about one thousand four hundred feet. They are said to
be of volcanic structure and are remarkable for the regu-
larity of the sky line which they present in many places.
As we departed from the coast the appearance of the
country became more attractive. A stunted growth of
spruce covered the hills and a thick mantle of firs and moss
softened the outlines of the rocky islands. Owing to continuous calms, our progress was provokingly slow and
ample opportunity was given for sketching and studying
the country. To the north, extended a rolling, hilly region
monotonous in comparison with the bolder country to the
south. As we approached the western end of the bay,
however, a conspicuous peak was seen rising from a chain
of hills about ten miles from the north shore of the bay.
This mountain, which is called Makaumé by the Hudson's
Bay Company officials, from its isolation as well as its
height, dominates the entire surrounding country, forming
a conspicuous landmark for many miles. I subsequently

learned from the Mountaineer Indians that their name for this mountain is Pootakabooshkow (that which rises up). They endow this eminence with the same supernatural attributes which their brethren of the southwest ascribe to the great rock of Lake Mistassini ; and, when passing near, on no account can they be persuaded to point or refer to it, believing such ill conduct the inevitable fore-runner of stormy weather and misfortune.

We arrived at North-west River Post at the head of the Bay, on July 27th. This is the most inland station of the Hudson's Bay Company on the Atlantic seaboard, and is the chief trading point of the Montagnais or Mountain-eer Indians, who make annual visits to this post to meet the Roman Catholic missionary, and to exchange the out-come of their winter's trapping for supplies and ammuni-tion. Many of the Indians had already visited the post and returned to the interior, but quite a number were still encamped in the neighborhood. The Grand River flows into the bay twenty-five miles from here, and at this point preparations were made to ascend the river. I was con-vinced that the proper method of ascending the Grand River, a swift-flowing stream abounding in rapids, was to secure a number of canoes and Indians to man them. With two large canoes in addition to our own, and a crew of natives acquainted with the country, we were prepared to attempt the difficulties of river navigation, with a fair prospect of achieving the object of the trip. A serious disappointment, as far as this part of our plan was con-cerned, was in store for us. A whole week was wasted in the vain endeavor to secure Indian guides and helpers in our enterprise. In addition to their disinclination to engage in an undertaking involving so much hard work, we found that a superstitious dread of the Falls obtained

NORTHWEST RIVER POST.   FROM A PHOTOGRAPH.

among them. They firmly believe the place to be the
haunt of evil spirits, and assert that death will soon over-
take the venturesome mortal who dares to look upon the
mysterious cataract.

While at Rigolet, I had the pleasure of meeting Père
Lemoine, the French Canadian missionary, who was
returning from his annual visit to the Indians at North-
west River. He gave me much information about the
Indians, and talked most entertainingly of his work. Soon
after reaching the post, in company with an interpreter, I
visited a camp of the Indians on Grand Lake with the
object of securing a crew for my river journey. On leaving Rigolet, Père Lemoine had handed me a letter to the
Indians, written in their own language and accompanied
with a translation. In this communication he commended
me in the most simple and dignified terms to the members
of his roaming flock, and invoked their aid in helping me
on my journey. In spite of this credential, however, I
found, after a two hours' interview, that it would be out
of the question to look for aid in this quarter, as no induce-
ments I could hold out were strong enough to overcome
their objections to the undertaking.

According to a census taken by the Newfoundland
Government in 1891, the entire population of Labrador on
the east coast from Blanc Sablon to Cape Chudleigh num-
bered but four thousand one hundred, and this doubtless
included Indians, Eskimos, Whites and Half-breeds. The
Eskimos live on the coast, and seldom venture far into the
interior. Hamilton Inlet may be regarded as the southern
boundary of their habitat, which stretches north to the
shores of Hudson Strait. Contact with civilization seems
to lessen the vitality of this interesting race, and the
Moravian missionaries declare that, like the Eskimos of

Alaska, they are gradually decreasing in numbers. The great inland plateau, dotted with innumerable lakes, is the home of the Indians. These belong to the Cree nation of the north-west, and are divided into two families: the Montagnais, or Mountaineers, who are found as far west as Lake St. John in the Province of Quebec, and the Nascopies, a less numerous tribe, who dwell on the barren grounds extending to the far north.

All the Indians in this part of Labrador are nominally Roman Catholics; but as the ministrations of the priest extend over a period of only three weeks each year—during which all marriages and baptisms are solemnized—there is time in the long interval for many of the precepts of the Church to be forgotten and for inherent superstition to assert itself. The heathen element is exemplified in the survival of the native "medicine men" or "conjurors," as they are termed, who undoubtedly wield much influence over their followers. The priest exerts himself to lessen the authority of this savage hierachy; but it is well known that, away from his watchful care, the old barbaric incanta-

Copyright, 1892, by THE CENTURY Co.

SKETCH MAP OF GRAND RIVER LABRADOR

C.A.KENASTON,1891

SCALE OF MILES

The figures show elevations above the surface of the river in feet

tions and prophecies are still practised.[10]   For many years past, the sale of spirituous liquors to the Indians has been interdicted, and they possess many of the virtues of isolated native communities, while their proficiency in reading and writing their native language is extraordinary, when their limited opportunities are taken into consideration.   These Labrador Indians are specimens of a primitive race who show but few evidences of contact with white men.   In fact, aside from the priest and the local representative of the Company, they rarely encounter any white men, and their mode of life and customs present many aspects of interest to the ethnologist.   The caribou, or reindeer, furnishes the chief item of their food supply, and likewise provides them with covers for their wigwams and material for clothing.   The winter of 1890-91 was notable for the great scarcity of this animal and a consequent famine among the Indians of this part of Labrador.

A vast extent of territory is covered by these natives in their wanderings.   Small companies, consisting of three or four families, usually travel together.   In summer, their

---

[10] A Labrador correspondent, under date of August 13, 1893, informs me that the Roman Catholic mission to the Indians at North-west River, for many years under the care of the Oblate Fathers, has recently been abandoned.

birch-bark canoes traverse the rivers and the chains of lakes which extend in all directions. In winter, they wander about in pursuit of game and engage in trapping, travelling over the snow on their cumbersome, circular snow-shoes, and dragging their toboggan-shaped sledges behind them. Early marriages are the rule among them, eighteen being the average age of the men, while the women are usually two years younger when they assume the responsibilities of matrimony.

Unlike most Indian tribes, the Mountaineers, as far as I have been able to learn, have but elementary ideas of self-government, and hereditary or elective chiefs do not exist among them. The explanation of this may be found in their exemption from wars for many generations. Traditions of conflicts with the Eskimos still exist among them, and it is reasonable to suppose that chiefs were recognized among them at that time in their history.[11]

The Nascopies, who dwell about the lacustrine basins of the northern part of the inland plateau, are closely allied to the Mountaineers in language and habits, but are a more hardy and primitive people. Their clothing is entirely composed of deer-skins, and many have no intercourse whatever with white men. Numbers of them, however, make annual visits to Fort Chimo, the station of the Hudson's Bay Company near Ungava Bay, where, in exchange for their pelts, they obtain flour, ammunition and a few other articles. With these products of civilization they fortify themselves in the battle with nature which mere existence in those sterile regions implies. The for-

---

[11] Eskimo Island, twelve miles west of Rigolet, in Melville Bay, is pointed out as being the scene of the last great battle between these hereditary enemies. Eskimo graves and the remains of rude breastworks are still to be found there. Tradition holds that the battle resulted in the defeat of the Eskimos.

mer Roman Catholic missionary, Père Lecasse, on two occasions extended his journeys as far north as Fort Chimo, in order to meet the Nascopies who resorted there for trade ; but it is said the principles of Christianity have made but little headway among them. I am informed by one who spent two years at this Fort, that the savage custom of killing the aged and helpless still prevails among the Nascopies. The victim is not despatched outright, however, but is supplied with sufficient food to last a few days and is then abandoned to a cruel death by starvation.

Thwarted in our plan of Indian coöperation, we nevertheless resolved to make the best of the situation, and our party on starting up the river comprised, besides Prof. Kenaston and myself, John Montague and Geoffrey Ban.

Montague, a strong young Scotchman, proved to be a valuable addition to our party. Emigrating from the Orkney Islands when a boy, he had for years followed the life of a " planter;" that is, had engaged in the fisheries during the summer and trapped in the winter, drawing his supplies from the Hudson's Bay Company and trading exclusively with them. He accompanied Mr. Holme on his journey in 1887, and was well acquainted with the lower part of the river. Geoffrey was a full-blooded Eskimo, twenty-five years old, born at Okkak on the north eastern coast. He was a typical specimen of his race and closely resembled the more primitive members of the Eskimo family, whom I subsequently encountered in north Greenland in the summer of 1892. Of strong and stocky build, he possessed likewise a swarthy, Tartar cast of features, and a cheerfulness of disposition which the vicissitudes of travel seldom ruffled.

2

A strong river boat, eighteen feet in length, was obtained for the trip, and in this were placed the supplies, instruments and other necessary luggage for the journey. The canoe containing the tent and a few smaller articles, was tied to the stern.

On August 3d, our little company bade adieu to Mr. Charles McLaren, the officer in charge of North-west River Post, and turned our faces towards the wilderness. After advancing a distance of fifteen miles to the south, an adverse wind arose and we camped for the night on Rabbit Island, in Goose Bay, five miles from the mouth of Grand River.

The following day, after a sail of an hour and a half, we entered the river, which at its mouth, is over a mile in width. The shores of Goose Bay are quite low at this point, and the approach is not impressive. Vast quantities of sand and *débris* are washed down by the river in the spring, and sand bars form at the mouth, making it difficult to follow a continuous channel for any length of time. Partly submerged stumps and logs appeared at intervals. There is an appreciable tide at the mouth of the river, but the rise and fall does not usually exceed two feet. Passing Man-of-War Island and the mouth of Travispines River, a stiff easterly wind bore us swiftly along, and a total distance of twenty-five miles was covered before we made camp. For the first fifteen miles steep sand banks characterized both sides of the river.

As we rowed up stream the next day, the northern shore presented steep banks of whitish clay, whose sides were furrowed by rain channels. Along the shore, curious clay concretions, in grotesque shapes, were found in profusion, the result, possibly, of the union of the sand in suspension in the river and the kaoline soil carried by erosive agencies

PART OF THE LOWER OR MIDDLE FALLS OF THE GRAND RIVER. (FROM A PHOTOGRAPH.)

into the stream.   Interesting little creatures, called jump-
ing mice (Zaphus Hudsonius), were observed in the vicinity; but they carefully avoided the traps set for them.

By noon we arrived at the base of the lower falls of
the river, called Muskrat Falls by the trappers.   Just
above this point the Grand River swings around from the
north and forms a basin over half a mile in width.   At
the lower end of this, a chain of hills encroaches on the
bed of the river, contracting the channel and presenting a
rocky bulwark, through which the stream has forced its
course.   There are two steps in the descent, and the total
drop to the falls was ascertained to be sixty-six feet, while
the width of the narrow rapid between the upper and lower
fall was found by Prof. Kenaston to be three hundred and
twenty feet.

To circumvent the falls a difficult "carry" was necessary, involving a steep ascent of two hundred and ten
feet, then a trail of half a mile through a forest of birch
and spruce trees, and finally an abrupt descent to the
river.

The unwieldy character of our boat, which weighed
over five hundred pounds, was now a serious disadvantage.
By means of a block and tackle we dragged it up the precipitous banks, and after much laborious lifting and pull-
ing, launched it on the river above the falls.   This opera-
tion, and the "packing" of the "stuff" across, occupied a
day and a half.   During our subsequent advance of about
one hundred and seventy-five miles up the river, oars and
paddles were, for the most part, of little use, owing to the
swiftness of the current.   The only exceptions were along
a part of the river known as "Slackwater," and on Lake
Wanakopow, where we enjoyed the luxury of a sail for
forty miles.   The usual method employed was what is

technically known as "tracking." That is, a strong rope, about the thickness of a clothes-line, was tied to the gunwale of the boat just aft of the bow. To the shore end of this broad leather straps were attached. With these across their shoulders, three of the party tugged away along the rocky bank, while number four of our crew, with an oar lashed in the stern, steered a devious course among the rocks and shallows of the river. The " tow-path " in this instance was of the roughest and most diversified character. Sandy terraces and extended reaches covered with glacial boulders characterized the lower portion of the river, while further up stream, great numbers of smaller boulders, insecurely lodged on the precipitous sandy banks, would baffle us by the precarious footing they afforded. Where a combination of this "rubble" and a troublesome rapid occurred, it was only by the most violent exertion and no end of slipping and sliding that the tension of the tow-line could be maintained on the treacherous ground. Then, again, stretches of steep rocky bank, where no tracking was possible, would often compel us to scale the rugged cliffs and pass the line from one to another over various obstacles. Wading through the water was frequently the only resource. This was always the case when we reached a place in the river where the spring freshets had undermined the banks, and where numbers of trees, stumps and underbrush littered the shore, forming *chevaux-de-frise* of the most formidable character.

The long daylight of midsummer in this subarctic region was a point in our favor, enabling us to work to the limit of our strength. Here, indeed, we found that " Night and day hold each other's hands upon the hill-tops. . . .

No sooner does the sun set north by west, then, like a giant refreshed, it rises again north by east."[12]

On the fourth day from the mouth of the river, we passed Porcupine Rapids without difficulty, having ascended a distance of fifty-seven miles. Our camp for the evening was in a pleasant grove recently vacated by the Indians. Here we found a number of the curious wicker frames which the natives use in bathing. These frames are covered with deer-skins and are erected over holes in the ground, into which a number of large stones, previously heated, are rolled. The bather is then placed within, and water thrown on the stones, thus creating an intensely hot vapor. Forests of evergreens extended back on both sides, and a notable increase in the size of the firs and spruces was observed as we advanced into the interior. Deposits of magnetic iron ore sand were observed on the banks of the river here as well as elsewhere in the lower part of its course. On August 9th, we reached the head of Gull Island Lake, which is nothing but a widening of the river. The lake is a favorite resort of the Canada goose, and its waters contain large numbers of white fish, pickerel and suckers. Above Gull Island Lake, the valley of the river contracts gradually; the sandy terraces disappear, and sloping banks, strewn with erratics, are encountered for many miles.

The next day, when a few miles above the lake, we beheld the white crests of Gull Island Rapids ahead of us. This was one of the dangerous points in our course, and we approached it with caution, taking advantage of eddies along the shore, where a reverse current often aided our

[12] Lambert de Boilieu. *Recollections of Labrador Life.* London. 1861.

advance. The successful rounding of a point or the sur-
mountal of a bad rapid was always attended with excite-
ment. The canoe capsized at one point; but as the con-
tents were lashed in, nothing was lost by the accident.
We found it impossible to drag the heavily-loaded boat
against the current at another place, and were compelled
to unload and carry the stores around the worst part of the
rapid. On this day we made but four miles. The current
was now uniformly swift, running at about eight miles an
hour. Parts of two days were consumed in conquering
Horseshoe Rapid, which is divided into three distinct
rapids.

On August 13th, we passed the Ninnipi Rapids. These
compare with Gull Island Rapids in difficulty, and necessitated detaching the canoe and " packing " the boat's freight
along shore as in the previous instance.

Judged by ordinary standards of travel, our advance
up the river was slow indeed; but to those who are fa-
miliar with canoe transportation on Canadian rivers, I am
sure our progress will appear respectable, when the un-
wieldly character of our boat is taken into consideration.
There seems to be something positively personal and vin-
dictive in the resistance which rapids make to a traveller's
advance into a wild and mountainous country. There was,
accordingly, a cumulative feeling of satisfaction as one
after another of these barriers of nature's making were
surmounted. In the swollen condition of the river, the
struggle with these wild rapids was often as savage and
exhilarating as one could desire. John and myself usually
took the lead on the tow-line, Geoffrey busying himself
with keeping the line clear of snags, while to Prof.
Kenaston was assigned the steersman's part. Bending to
their work, the linemen would clamber along the bank,

PACKING ROUND THE SEMAPHORES. FROM A PHOTOGRAPH.

dragging the slowing yielding mass up stream. Ofttimes
the force of the current would carry out the boat far into
mid-stream, until the full length of line would be exhausted.
We could do nothing then ; but hang on like grim death
and watch our craft toss and roll amid the billows, until,
like a spirited horse, gradually yielding to the strain, she
would turn her head shorewards. Prof. Kenaston mean-
while, with tense muscles bending to the steering oar,
skilfully guided his charge amid the encompassing
rocks and eddies—the only quiet figure on the surging
flood of the river. At the Ninnipi Rapids the stream narrows perceptibly, and the mountains, covered with a dense
growth of burnt timber, reach to the water's edge. The
Ninnipi River here enters the Grand River from the south-
west, and forms part of a canoe route used by the Indians
in going to the Gulf of St. Lawrence. On August 14th,
we traversed a portion of the river which Montague called
Slackwater. Here, owing to the long stretches of smooth
water, and infrequent rapids, rowing became practicable,
and a distance of twenty miles was covered in two days.
For a good portion of this distance the adjacent hills were
covered with burnt timber, which gave a sombre aspect to
the landscape.

The current now became swifter and the tracking more
arduous. On August 18th, the canoe capsized twice
while dragging behind the boat. On the second of these
occasions, when in the midst of a stubborn rapid, the
weight of the submerged canoe and the heavy boat proved
to be too much for the strong tracking line, and it broke,
treating the steersman to an involuntary ride down stream
for several hundred yards. On August 19th, the Mouni
Rapids showed their troubled waters ahead of us. These
were the last ones of a formidable nature we encountered,

and owing to the swollen condition of the river they gave
us a hard tussle before they were conquered. They extend
over a longer distance than any of the others, and the
aneroid readings which I recorded from time to time
showed a greater drop here in the bed of the river than at
any other point.

Looking back on these days spent along the river, I
recall how each one was filled with incident and how all
were stimulated by the uncertainty of what lay before us.
It is the experience of many, that in recalling travels of
this kind, the pleasant features of the time are remem-
bered with more distinctness than the trying ones. So in
the retrospect of this journey, many of the incidents,
unpleasant at the time, are softened by time's perspective,
while the bright ones stand out in bolder relief and recur to
the memory with pleasure. One awkward adventure,
however, which occurred on this first day on the Mouni
Rapids, I have not yet succeeded in relegating to the
realm of forgetfulness. We were approaching a rocky
point, similar to many others we had encountered, past
which the water dashed with angry violence. It was our
custom on reaching such a place, to first detach the canoe,
and then to shove out the boat obliquely from the still
water, to allow her bow to fairly meet the swifter current.
On this occasion, while Montague and I, facing up stream,
were waiting on the bank above for the signal to advance, the boat, through some carelessness, was pushed
out from the quiet eddy squarely into the swift water.
The full force of the torrent struck her abeam, and away
she swept down stream like a thing possessed. Taken
unawares, no time was given to throw off the leather
straps from our shoulders, and instantly we were thrown
from our feet and dragged over the rocks into the river by

the merciless strength of the flood. Most fortunately for me, the circular strap slipped over my head, as I was being dragged through the water. Montague's also released itself, and the runaway sped down stream a quarter of a mile before stopping. On clambering up the bank, I found Montague stunned and bleeding from a scalp wound. Aside from some abrasions of the skin, I was none the worse for the shaking up, and after a brief delay Montague revived and we resumed our " tow-path " exercise.

The popular impression that Labrador possesses a climate which even in summer is too rigorous for the enjoyment of open-air life, was not verified on this trip. The temperature during the day was found to be delightful—just cool enough to be stimulating ; while the average minimum temperature registered during the forty-one nights of the journey was ascertained to be but forty-two degrees Fahrenheit. Nor was verdure lacking in this sub-arctic landscape, for dense growths of spruce and fir extended back for miles into the blue distance, and even where fire had blackened the slopes of adjacent hills, the sombre aspect of the scene was much relieved by a second growth, which showed the delicate green of its leaves among the charred remains of the original forest. Game and fish proved to be fairly abundant, and two fine black bears were killed by members of the party. The fresh meat thus obtained, together with the trout captured from time to time, made welcome variations in the dietary of the expedition.

The declining sun of August 20th beheld our small craft glide into the smooth waters of Lake Wanakopow. The first view of the lake was beautiful, and most grateful to our eyes after the long struggle with the rapids. Even Geoffrey and John, usually indifferent to scenic effects,

could not conceal their admiration as we glided by tower-
ing cliffs and wooded headlands, and beheld at intervals
cascades leaping from the rocks into the lake, their silvery
outlines glistening in the sun and contrasting distinctly
with the environment of dark evergreen foliage. This
romantic sheet of water stretches in a north-easterly and
south-westerly direction a distance of about thirty-five
miles, and has an elevation above sea level, according to
my aneroid observations, of four hundred and sixty-
two feet. Low mountains of granite and gneiss rise on
both sides, and the average width of the lake is less than
one mile. A sounding taken near the middle showed a
depth of four hundred and six feet. This narrow elevated basin is probably of glacial origin, the presence of
great numbers of boulders and the rounded appearance of
the hill summits, pointing to a period of ice movement.
On Saturday, August 22d, we made a good run up the
lake, passing Mr. Holme's farthest point, and camped on
the river bank three miles above the lake, opposite the
mouth of the Elizabeth River, which here enters the
Grand from the west. The next day we rested in camp;
taking occasion to overhaul our boat and canoe and repair
clothing and outfit, preparatory to entering the *terra incognita* which lay before us. The following day we made ten
miles, there being but little current to contend against.
The river retained its width to a marked degree, and frequent placid expanses, having all the appearance of mountain lakes, revealed themselves as we turned the bends of
the stream. About ten miles above the lake a very considerable river flows in from the east. On subsequent
inquiry from the Indians, I was unable to learn of the
existence of any native name for this stream. On August
25th, a cold rain poured down all day, but the river pre-

sented no special difficulties, and we made eleven miles progress. Thirteen miles more were covered the following day, the water meantime becoming more shallow and lofty hills arising from the shore.

We had now reached a point over fifty miles above the middle of Lake Wanakopow, where Mr. Holme had been obliged to turn back. On his map he places the Grand Falls thirty miles above the lake, and represents the river as approaching the lake from a point west of south from the lake itself. We had ascertained that the river entered the lake from the west, instead of from the south-west, and we were likewise forced to realize that Mr. Holme was mistaken in his location of the Falls, as we had already reached a point considerably beyond their assumed position. On August 27th, after advancing three miles, we came to a wide, shallow rapid, over which it was impossible to draw the boat. Finding no possible channel in the river, we judged that we were in the neighborhood of the "Big Hill," the head of boat navigation and the point where the Indian *voyageurs* left the river, in the old days when the Hudson's Bay Company sent crews to their inland post.

While at the North-west River Post we had learned from a reliable Indian, that the old trail, long disused, led from this point on the river to a chain of lakes on the table-land. By following these lakes and crossing the intervening "carries," the rapid water which extends for twenty-five miles below the Falls could be circumvented and the traveller brought finally to the waters of the Grand River, many miles above the Grand Falls. Our plan was to follow this old trail for several days, and then to leave the canoe and strike across country in a direction which we hoped would bring us again to the river in the vicinity of the Falls. It was deemed best to follow this circuitous canoe route, rather than to attempt to follow the banks of the river on foot, in which case everything would have to be carried on our backs through dense forests for many miles.

After a long search, the old trail was found, and leaving Geoffrey in charge of the main camp on the river, the other members of the party took the canoe and a week's provisions, and began the ascent of the steep path which led up to the edge of the elevated plateau, which here approaches the river. Making a "carry" of three miles to the north along the old trail, we reached the first of the chain of lakes, where we erected a rude shelter and camped for the night. A violent storm arose during the night, and next day we lost much time in seeking for the continuation of the trail on the opposite side of the lake. Having been disused for twenty-seven years, the path, where it came out on the lake shore, was distinguished by no "blazes" on the trees, or recent choppings. This necessitated a careful examination of the shores on all the lakes, and caused considerable delay.

We were now on the great table-land of the Labrador interior, and wishing to get a good outlook, climbed a conspicuous hill nearby, to scan the adjacent country: A view truly strange and impressive was before us. As far as the eye could reach, extended an undulating country, sparsely covered with stunted spruce trees, among which great weather-worn rocks gleamed, while on all sides white patches of caribou moss gave a snowy effect to the scene. A hundred shallow lakes reflected the fleeting clouds above, their banks lined with boulders, and presenting a labyrinth of channels and island passages. Low hills arose at intervals among the bogs and lakes; but the

general effect of the landscape was that of flatness and
bleak monotony.

The continuation of the old Nascopie trail remaining
invisible, to escape the discomfort of another rainy night
on the plateau, we returned to the shelter of the camp on
the river. On August 30th, we returned to Geoffrey Lake,
where our patient search for the trail was at last successful.

Next day we advanced along the trail which led us
over four " carries " and across five lakes. For convenience
of reference, we applied names to some of these small sheets
of water. Thus, the third one of the chain was designated
" Gentian Lake," from finding the closed variety of the blue
gentian growing on its borders. The next day we turned
aside from the dim trail and paddled to the north-western
extremity of the sixth lake, where we drew the canoe ashore
and prepared for the tramp across country. Arrayed in
heavy marching order, and carrying nearly all that
remained of our provisions, we were soon advancing westward on a course which we hoped would soon bring us to
the river in the vicinity of the Falls. The country we were
now passing through was of the most desolate character,
denuded of trees and the surface covered with caribou
moss, Labrador tea plants, blueberry bushes, and thousands
of boulders. By keeping to the ridges, fair progress was
made ; but when compelled to leave the higher ground and
skirt the borders of the lakes, dense thickets of alders and
willows were encountered, and these greatly impeded our
advance. Language seems inadequate to describe the desolation of this upland landscape. No living thing was
encountered, and the silence of primordial time reigned
supreme.

Just before sunset we went into camp on a hillside
near a large lake, and soon after, from the top of a high

rock, beheld a great column of mist rising like smoke
against the western sky. This we knew marked the position of the Falls, and needless to say, our spirits rose—
oblivious of our bleak surroundings—as we contemplated
the near attainment of our journey's end. During the
night the thermometer registered a minimum temperature
of forty-one degrees, and we were treated to a superb dis-
play of Northern Lights.

September 2d was a day memorable as marking the
date of our arrival at the Grand Falls. A rough march
over the rocks and bogs intervened, however, before we
reached this goal. As we approached the river, spruce forests of a heavier growth appeared, and pressing on through
these, although we could no longer see the overhanging
mist, the deep roar of falling waters was borne to our ears
with growing distinctness. After what seemed an intol-
erable length of time—so great was our eagerness—a space
of light in the trees ahead made known the presence of the
river. Quickening our steps, we pushed on, and with
beating hearts emerged from the forest near the spot where
the river plunged into the chasm with a deafening roar.

A single glance showed that we had before us one of
the greatest waterfalls in the world. Standing at the
rocky brink of the chasm, a wild and tumultuous scene
lay before us, a scene possessing elements of sublimity
and with details not to be apprehended in the first
moments of wondering contemplation. Far up stream
one beheld the surging, fleecy waters and tempestuous billows, dashing high their crests of foam, all forced onward
with resistless power towards the steep rock, whence they
took their wild leap into the deep pool below. Turning to
the very brink and looking over, we gazed into a world of
mists and mighty reverberations. Here the exquisite

VIEW OF THE RAPIDS NEAR THE BRINK OF THE GREAT FALLS. FROM A PHOTOGRAPH.

colors of the rainbow fascinated the eye, and majestic
sounds of falling waters continued the pean of the ages.
Below and beyond the seething caldron the river appeared,
pursuing its turbulent career, past frowning cliffs and over
miles of rapids, where it heard " no sound save its own
dashings." The babel of waters made conversation a
matter of difficulty, and after a mute exchange of con-
gratulations, we turned our attention to examining the
river in detail above and below the Falls.

A mile above the main leap, the river is a noble stream
four hundred yards wide, already flowing at an accelerated
speed. Four rapids, marking successive depressions in
the river bed, intervene between this point and the Falls.
At the first rapid the width of the stream is not more than
one hundred and seventy-five yards, and from thence
rapidly contracts until reaching a point above the escarpment proper, where the entire column of fleecy water is
compressed within rocky banks not more than fifty yards
apart.

Here the effect of resistless power is extremely fine.
The maddened waters sweeping downwards with terrific
force, rise in great surging billows high above the encompassing banks ere they finally hurl themselves into the
gulf below. A great pillar of mist rises from the spot, and
numerous rainbows span the watery abyss, constantly
forming and disappearing amid the clouds of spray. An
immense volume of water precipitates itself over the rocky
ledge, and under favorable conditions the roar of the
cataract can be heard for twenty miles. Below the falls,
the river turning to the south-east, pursues its maddened
career for twenty-five miles shut in by vertical cliffs of
gneissic rock which rises in places to a height of four hundred feet. The rocky banks above and below the falls

are thickly wooded with firs and spruces, among which
the graceful form of the white birch appears in places.

Soon after our arrival, Prof. Kenaston, with Montague's aid, set about making a measurement of the falls.
In an address delivered before the National Geographic
Society, January 29, 1892, Prof. Kenaston described the
method employed as follows: "At St. Johns, Newfoundland, we had provided ourselves with several balls of
stout linen cord with which to measure the height of the
fall, if the situation should be found suitable. Fortunately,
alongside the chute just above the brink of the main cataract, we found a floor of rock of the same slope, about
thirty degrees below the horizontal. Along this it was
possible to go, but with some peril, nearly to the edge
over which the stream plunges in its final descent. Fasten-
ing a heavy billet of green fir to one end of the cord, the
weight was carried and thrown down on the surface of the
rock to the brink of the falls, the cord being paid out from
the upper end of the slope. A knot was made in the cord
to mark the distance to the edge, and the billet was
allowed to fall over the edge of the precipice into the
chasm. Montague, having climbed along the bank at the
edge of the cañon, was holding on by the trunk of a tree,
from which he could see when the block of wood struck
the water below as the cord was paid out by me above.
The instant of contact was plainly visible to him, and
and I was equally sensible of it. The cord was now drawn
up over the edge and carefully measured with a tape-line.
The whole length paid out was five hundred and five feet,
the part which measured the slope was one hundred and
eighty-nine feet, leaving for the height of the main fall
below the chute, three hundred and sixteen feet. Allowing
for a few degrees deviation from the perpendicular, and for

a slight stretching of the cord, though this last was probably counteracted by wetting, the height of the fall may be considered something more than three hundred feet. The vertical height of the chute, about thirty-two feet added to the other measurement, makes the descent from the head of the chute to the surface of the water in the chasm about three hundred and forty-eight feet."

While Prof. Kenaston and Montague were making this direct measurement of the Falls, an incident occurred which illustrated the cool daring of the latter in a striking manner. The water, at the time of our visit, was probably as low as it ever is in the Grand River. In fact, from the *débris* lodged high up on the banks, we judged the stream had fallen at least ten feet from the high-water mark of the spring freshets. This drop in the river left exposed a considerable surface of the rocky ledge which was usually covered by water, forming part of the brink of the fall. After measuring the length of the preliminary incline leading to the main leap, Montague was directed to cast the plummet-line over the rocky edge of the escarpment, in order to secure the measurement of the principal fall. This was done; but while Prof. Kenaston was paying out the line, it caught in a slight crevice, and to complete the measurement it became necessary to free it at once. Without a moment's hesitation, our brave John clambered down the steep bank and walked out on the very brink of the chasm, where, stooping down, with the spray of the passing flood wetting his cheek, he loosened the line and returned to the bank in safety. A single misstep or the slightest giddiness on his part, while on that dizzy height, would have resulted tragically. But to think was to act with this hardy Scotchman, and, truly, his cool head and nerve served him well on this occasion.

3

While these direct measurements were being made, I turned my attention to obtaining a number of photographs of the falls and rapids, and then to securing the barometric readings above and below the cataract. In order to obtain an observation at the lower bed of the river, it was necessary to descend the steep walls of the cañon. This I found to be a hazardous and exciting undertaking. Walking along the edge of the gorge just below the falls, two places seemed to offer possible means of access to the river below. At both points I attempted the descent, only to find, after lowering myself 'from tree to tree down the bank, that a sheer precipice extended the remaining fifty or seventy-five feet to the surface of the water. On the third trial, by following the course of a tiny streamlet the bed of the river was finally reached. By this time the day was far spent, and darkness almost enveloped the scene down in that imprisoned channel bed. The situation was interesting, and filled with the charm of a first glimpse into one of nature's solitudes. In front, the great river, roaring hoarsely in the gloom, and just entering on its final journey over miles of rapids to the sea. On the opposite bank, a splendid cliff of pinkish hue led the eye from the gloomy base, in one long sweep hundreds of feet aloft to the utmost pinnacle, which still glowed a few brief moments in the departing rays of the sun.

The aneroid reading and the temperature recorded, a few minutes were given to contemplating the strange beauty of the scene, and then began the toilsome climb to the upper world. Darkness had settled over all when I clambered over the edge above and made my way through the forest to the camp, just above the falls. My long absence had alarmed my companions, who welcomed my appearance within the circle of the camp-fire with expres-

RAPIDS ABOVE THE GRAND FALLS.—FROM A PHOTOGRAPH TAKEN 250 FEET ABOVE THE FALLS

sions of relief. It was after nine o'clock when I sat down
to a frugal supper that night, somewhat footsore and weary
after the stirring events of the day.

The difficulties of obtaining near views of large
masses of falling water are admitted by all photogra-
phers. In the case of the Grand Falls, this is increased
by the character of the surroundings. The great volume
of water compressed as it is, and discharging itself through
a funnel-like channel in the rocks, falls in a thick narrow
column a distance of three hundred and sixteen feet, sending up banks of vapor and presenting the appearance from
a distance of a great pillar of cloud. The vegetation is
affected by this vapory condition of the atmosphere, and
thin patches of green moss, unlike anything seen elsewhere, were conspicuous on the face of the cliffs just
below the Falls. Notwithstanding the apparent futility of
the attempt, I endeavored to obtain two views looking
across the main leap, from the bank near the brink. These
negatives proved to be failures on development. By
descending the bank as far as the steep incline per-
mitted and hanging to the roots of the dwarf fir trees
growing thereabouts, I was able, by watching for a
favorable moment when the veil of mist lightened, to
secure a near view of part of the main leap. It was
apparent that the best vantage ground for viewing the
face of the Fall was from a point where the cañon wall
jutted out a short distance into the deep pool below the
Falls. This point of view I estimate was from one hundred
and fifty to two hundred feet from the column of descending
water, and down its rocky edge one could not creep more
than fifteen feet before encountering the almost vertical
wall which led to the river-bed below. While the rising
vapor did not envelope us here as when nearer the brink,

yet the effect of it, rising in banks from the base, while
not unpleasing to the eye, detracted somewhat from the
fine sweep of the Fall, the outline of which we could see
descending behind the veil of mist.   While on this rocky
buttress, I took a photograph of the Falls and one of the
lower part of the Falls, showing the mist rising from the
bottom, both of which proved to be far from satisfactory.

To explain further the lack of definition in those
photographs, I will add that the afternoon was far advanced
when they were taken and the light far from good.   The
sun was already well down in the western sky, across the
river from me, and in the worst possible position for my
purpose.   I emphasize this feature of the occasion, because
it materially affected the result; for had the sun shone
from the south instead of the west, I think it would have
been quite possible to secure a view showing at least the
outline of the Falls.   On the afternoon in question, however, the conditions were quite the contrary, hence the
unsatisfactory results.

In my descent to the bottom of the cañon I carried
my camera, but I was unable to obtain a view of the fall
from the lower bed of the river, because a projecting point
of rock several hundred yards up-stream cut off a distant
view of the spectacle.   The steep walls of the gorge,
against which the water dashed in places, prevented any
considerable advance up-stream, and I was reluctantly
compelled to abandon my purpose of returning the following morning to secure photographs of the Falls from this
lower position.

I felt at the time that while the view of the rapids and
cañon promised well, those of the fall could not be other-
wise than unsatisfactory.   I consoled myself, however, by
the thought that the morning light of the following day

would prove more propitious. Great was my disappointment, then, when the third of September dawned a dull
and threatening day. The notes in my journal, written at
the time, express my keen regret at the turn affairs had
taken.

Friends have naïvely remarked, when I expressed my
regret at not obtaining a good view of the main Falls,
" Why did you not remain encamped at the Falls until
you had secured satisfactory photographs of this most
important object?" Our provisions were all but exhausted, only enough remaining after breakfast for two
scanty meals. To have remained under the circumstances
seemed to risk starvation, for owing to the absence of all
game from the vicinity there appeared to be no means of
eking out our supplies by the usual devices of the woods-
man. Thus, I decided to delay no longer for clearing
weather; and the two days' storm which supervened
proved, I think, the wisdom of the step.

The deep, incessant roar of the cataract that night was
our lullaby as, stretched out under a rough "barricade,"
we glided into that realm of forgetfulness where even surroundings strange as ours counted as naught.

By the morning light we again viewed the wonders of
the place, and sought for some sign of the presence of bird
or animal in the vicinity; but not a track or the glint of
a bird's wing rewarded our quest, and this avoidance of the
place by the wild creatures of the forest seemed to add a
new element of severity to the eternal loneliness of the spot.

The Grand Falls of Labrador, with their grim environment of time-worn, archaic rocks, are one of the scenic wonders of this Western world, and if nearer civilization, would
be visited by thousands of travellers every year. They
are nearly twice as high as Niagara, and are only inferior

to that marvellous caratact in breadth and volume of water. One of their most striking characteristics is the astonishing leap into space which the torrent makes in discharging itself over its rocky barrier. From the description given of the rapid drop in the river-bed and coincident narrowing of the channel, one can easily understand that the cumulative energy expended in this final leap of the pent-up waters is truly titanic.

If a sub-stratum of softer rock existed here, as at Niagara, a similar " Cave of the Winds" would enable one to penetrate a considerable distance beneath the fall. The uniform structure of the rock, however, prevents any unequal disintegration, and thus the overarching sheet of water covers a nearly perpendicular wall, the base of which is washed by the waters of the lower river. In spite of the fact that no creature, except one with wings, could hope to penetrate this sub-aqueous chamber, the place is inhabited, if we are to believe the traditions of the Labrador Indians. Many years ago, so runs the tale, two Indian maidens, gathering firewood near the Falls, were enticed to the brink and drawn over by the evil spirit of the place. During the long years since then, these unfortunates have been condemned to dwell beneath the fall and forced to toil daily dressing deer-skins; until now, no longer young and beautiful, they can be seen betimes through the mist, trailing their white hair behind them and stretching out shrivelled arms towards any mortal who ventures to visit the confines of their mystic dwelling-place.

The Indian name for the Grand Falls—Pat-ses-che-wan —means "The Narrow Place Where the Water Falls." Like the native word Niagara—" Thunder of Waters,"— this Indian designation contains a poetic and descriptive quality which it would be hard to improve.

From the point where the river leaves the plateau and
plunges into the deep pool below the Falls, its course for
twenty-five miles is through one of the most remarkable
cañons in the world. From the appearance of the sides
of this gorge, and the zigzag line of the river, the indica-
tions are that the stream has slowly forced its way through
this rocky chasm, cutting its way back, foot by foot, from
the edge of the plateau to the present position of the Falls.
Recent investigators estimate that a period of six thousand
years was required to form the gorge below Niagara Falls;
or, in other words, that it has taken that time for the Falls
to recede from their former position at Queenstown
Heights to their present location. If it has taken this
length of time for the Niagara Falls to make their way
back a distance of seven miles by the erosive power of the
water acting on a soft shale rock supporting a stratum of
limestone, the immensity of time involved by assuming
that the Grand River cañon was formed in the same way
is so great that the mind falters in contemplating it, especially when it is recognized that the escarpment of the
Labrador Falls is of hard gneissic rock. And yet no other
explanation of the origin of this gorge is acceptable,
unless, indeed, we can assume that at some former time a
fissure occurred in the earth's crust as a result of igneous
agencies, and that this fissure ran in a line identical with
the present course of the river; in which case the drainage
of the table-land, collecting into the Grand River, would
follow the line of least resistance, and in the course of time
excavate the fissure into the present proportions of the
gorge.

The highest point reached by the expedition was in
the vicinity of the Falls, where, according to the aneroid
observations obtained, an elevation something in excess of

fifteen hundred feet was noted. Accepting the fact that
results obtained by the aneroid barometer are not regarded
as conclusive by careful observers, it is, nevertheless,
apparent that the altitudes obtained can be taken as at
least approximately correct, especially where it is borne in
mind that a standard instrument was used, and corrections
for temperature made in every instance. Thus it would
appear that the idea advanced by Prof. Hind and gen-
erally accepted, that the interior table-land of Labrador
attains a general elevation of over two thousand feet is
erroneous, and future travellers will be called on to con-
firm or reject this important point relating to the con-
figuration of the interior.

Having accomplished the main object of the trip, we
left a record of our visit on the river bank, and set out on
our return from this distant end of the expedition. A cold
rain poured down during the first day's tramp across the
barren plateau, and owing to a mistake in the course
taken, we missed our former track, and became entangled
in a lacustrine region, where we wandered for hours
unable to make any headway among the encompassing
lakes. In the humid air landmarks became indistinct, and
plunging on through bogs and over sharp rocks, cold, wet,
and wearied with the weight of our packs, and with
only enough flour remaining for one meal, our condition
was unpleasant in the extreme. But dismal thoughts of
being lost in this "great and terrible wilderness" incited
us to unusual efforts, and at length, by making a long
detour, a slight eminence was gained from which we could
pick out a course in the desired direction. Late in the
day we camped on a hillside under the shelter of a great
boulder. During the night the rain continued, accompanied by thunder and lightning, and towards morning a

high wind arose which demolished our " barricade " of sail-
cloth and brush. The most comfortless night of the
entire trip was passed in this camp on the bleak shores of
a lake on this cheerless table-land. Soon after daybreak
we each made a breakfast on a cup of hot tea, and resumed
our march towards the canoe.

After a rough scramble of nine miles, we arrived at
the lake, launched our canoe, and soon after fortified ourselves with a full meal. Returning through the chain of
lakes by the route we had recently used, we arrived in due
time at the camp on the river, where Geoffrey was await-
ing our return with some anxiety. Our trials were almost
ended when we reached the river ; and having embarked
on it, the swift current carried us down stream with
exhilarating speed. Delaying only long enough to make
a compass survey of the stream, in seven days the mouth
of the river was reached without serious mishap—a distance which required nearly a month's hard work in
ascending.

A series of fierce gales detained us a week at North-
west River, and we did not arrive at Rigolet until September 22d. Mr. Bell having kindly furnished us with a
small schooner, we proceeded in this to Indian Harbor, a
fishing station on the coast, where we had the good
fortune to find a Norwegian steamship which was about
to sail for St. Johns. We were soon established in com-
fortable quarters on board, and sailing the same day, made
a quick run to St. Johns, Newfoundland, from which point
I took a steamer to New York, where I arrived on October
15th; thus completing a journey of over four thousand
miles.

Among the results obtained by the expedition may
be mentioned the following : (1) The measurement of

the height of the Grand Falls. (2) Determination of the altitude of the table-land of south-eastern Labrador. (3) Map of lower course of the Grand River, from compass survey. (4) Meteorological observations extending over the six weeks of the journey. (5) Botanical collection illustrating Labrador flora. (6) Ethnological collection illustrating life and customs of mountaineer Indians and Eskimos.

During the journey we suffered some inconvenience from the absence of two commonplace articles—soap and baking powder; but the most serious affliction we were called on to endure arose from the endless persecution of the black flies and mosquitoes. These venemous insects are said to be worse in Labrador than in any other region, and their baneful presence greatly detracts from the enjoyment of summer travel in that country.

It is to be hoped that the attention of scientific travellers will be drawn to Labrador, which presents almost a virgin field to the investigator.[12] The shortness of the summer season and the sterility of the country preclude the successful tillage of the soil, and, in an agricultural sense, I can see no future for Labrador. But it is evident that the results of exploration in this isolated portion of North America would be of great value to geographical science, while it would not be at all strange if geological discoveries of commercial value would reward the enterprising pioneer in this new field of research.[13]

[12] Valuable and interesting results may be expected from the expedition sent out, in June, 1893, by the Geological and Natural History Survey of Canada, to explore the interior of Labrador. The leader of the expedition is Mr. A. P. Low, an experienced officer of the Survey, who proposes to be absent eighteen months, and to traverse the country north from Lake Mistassini to Ungava Bay and west from Hamilton Inlet to the shores of Hudson Bay.

[13] Prof. A. S. Packard (Mem. Boston Soc. of Nat. His., Vol. I), referring

THE CAÑON, A QUARTER OF A MILE BELOW THE GRAND FALL.

FROM A PHOTOGRAPH.

In closing, I take the liberty of quoting Dr. M. Harvey, who, in concluding a descriptive account of our journey, remarks : [14]

"It will be a long time before the Grand Falls of Labrador become a resort for ordinary tourists. Nature has placed this magnificent cataract in one of her deepest solitudes and guarded the approaches to it with jealous care. For unknown myriads of years its deep, thunderous diapason has been resounding through this grim wilderness. Thousands on thousands of years before the foundations of the Great Pyramid were laid, till the close of the glacial period, when the great ice-cap, three thousand feet thick, was lifted from Labrador, and its river systems were shaped, we must look for the genesis of the Grand Falls. When we look at the great chasm in the solid rock, twenty-five or thirty miles in length, and three hundred feet in depth, which this river has slowly excavated, as it cuts its way backward at the rate of a few feet in a century, we obtain some dim idea of the length of time that has elapsed since its waters began to flow. The imagination faints at the conception. What are we in comparison but ephemera of an hour. Man and all his works are but of yesterday when contrasted with this creation of the gray morning of time in the vast lonely land where desolation sits enthroned for evermore."

to a system of quartzite and trap rocks which extend along the coast about one hundred and twenty-five miles from Domino Harbor to Cape Webuc, gives an interesting account of these strata and remarks : "Should further search prove the existence, in connection with the quartzite of beds of a true conglomerate, which we should look for in the interior, and of the presence of copper ore in connection with quartz veins near the trap rocks, the identity of this formation with the Huronian rocks of Canada and similar rocks in Sweden would seem satisfactory ; and, if proven, will be interesting, not only to the geologist, but be of practical value in the search or ores on this coast."

[14] *New York Tribune. October 20, 1891.*

APPENDIX A.

ETHNOLOGICAL COLLECTION OBTAINED AT NORTH-WEST RIVER AND VICINITY, LABRADOR, AUGUST AND SEPTEMBER, 1891.

DEPOSITED IN THE NATIONAL MUSEUM, WASHINGTON, D.C.

MONTAGNAIS, OR MOUNTAINEER INDIANS.

Museum Number.

153,493. Prayer Book and Calendar, in native language.
153,494. Letter on Birch Bark, written by an Indian.
153,495. Beaming Tool, made from leg-bone of reindeer.
153,496. Woman's Cap, with bead ornaments.
153,497. Comb Case (*shecowan*) and Cleaner (*ousnac*).
153,498. Knife (*mohentagen*).
153,499. Awl (*pesemén*).
153,500. Grainer (*mechequat*), used in preparing skins.
153,501. Primitive form of Fish-Hook and Line.
153,502. Reindeer Sinew used as thread.
153,503. Woman's Work Bag (*menatis*), made from leg-skins of young reindeer.
153,504. Tool Bag (*oshatunas*).
153,505. Wallet for Gun Caps.
153,506-7. Moccasins.
153,508. Wallet with bead ornaments, used by women.
153,509. Snow-Shoes.
153,510. Conjuror's Drum.
153,511. Sled or Toboggan.
153,512. Photographs.

ESKIMOS—HAMILTON INLET AND VICINITY.

Museum
Number.

153,513. Woman's Work Bag.

153,514. Dog-Whip, 32½ feet long.

153,515. Native Drawing.

153,516. Boots made of Seal-skin.

153,517. Mitts for feet of sledge dog.

153,518. Woman's Coat of Seal-skin, with fox trimming.

153,519. Mittens, with fox-skin trimming.

153,520–22. Pouches of Seal-skin.

APPENDIX B.

LIST OF PLANTS OBTAINED ON GRAND RIVER EXPEDITION, AUGUST AND SEPTEMBER, 1891.

COLLECTED BY PROF. C. A. KENASTON.

Determined by the late Dr. G. Vasey, Department of Agriculture,
Washington, D. C.

[*Plants which have hitherto not been found in any existing catalogue of Labrador Flora, known to the author, are indicated by an asterisk.*]

RANUNCULACEÆ.

* Actæa alba, Bigel.

* Actæa spicata, L. var. rubra, Art.

* Aquilegia (undetermined).

SARRACENIACEÆ.

Sarracenia purpurea, L.

CARYOPHYLLACEÆ.

Arenaria peploides, L.

LEGUMINOSÆ.

Lathyrus maritimus, Bigel.

ROSACEÆ.

* Amelanchier.
* Fragaria Virginiana, Duchesne.
Potentilla Norvegica, L.
Potentilla palustris, Scop.
Potentilla tridentata, Sol.
Poterium Canadense, B. & H.
Prunus Pennsylvanica, Lf.
Rubus Chamæmorus, L.
Rubus triflorus, Richard.
* Rubus villosus, Ait.

SAXIFRAGACEÆ.

* Ribes rubrum, L.

ONAGRACEÆ.

Epilobium latifolium, L.

UMBELLIFERÆ.

Heracleum lanatum, Michx.

CORNACEÆ.

Cornus Canadensis, L.

CAPRIFOLIACEÆ.

Linnæa borealis, Gronov.

COMPOSITÆ.

Achillea Millefolium, L.
* Artemisia Canadensis, Michx.
* Aster acuminatus, Michx.
* Solidago humilis, Pursh.

ERICACEÆ.

Andromeda polifolia, L.
Chiogenes hispidula, T. & G.
Kalmia angustifolia, L.

Kalmia glauca, Ait.

Ledum latifolium, Art.

Pyrola chlorantha, Swartz.

* Pyrola elliptica, Nutt.

Pyrola secunda, L.

* Vaccinium Canadense, Kalm.

Vaccinium oxycoccus, L.

Vaccinium Vitis, Idæa, L.

GENTIANACEÆ.

Menyanthes trifoliata, L.

POLYGONACEÆ.

Polygonum viviparum, L.

* Rumex Acetosella, L.

SCROPHULARIACEÆ.

Castilleia pallida, Kunth, Var. septentrionalis, Gray.

SANTALACEÆ.

Commandra livida, Richards.

MYRICACEÆ.

* Myrica gale, L.

BETULACEÆ.

Alnus viridis, D. C.

Betula papyrifera, Mars.

SALICACEÆ.

* Salix lucida, Muhl.

EMPETRACEÆ.

Empetrum nigrum, L.

CONIFERÆ.

Juniperus communis, L.

Juniperus communis, Var. alpina, Gand.

Picea alba, Link.

IRIDACEÆ.

Iris Hookeri, Penny.

LILIACEÆ.

Clintonia borealis, Raf.
* Smilacina bifolia, D. C.
* Smilacina racemosa, Desf.
Streptopus roseus, Michx.

JUNCACEÆ.

* Juncus Balticus, Dethard.
* Juncus trifidus, L.

CYPERACEÆ.

Carex canescens, L., var., alpicola, Wahl.
Eriophorum russeolum, Fries.
* Scirpus sylvaticus, L.

GRAMINEÆ.

* Elymus arenarius, L.
Elymus mollis, Trin.
* Calamagrostis Canadensis (Hook.), Beauv.
* Calamagrostis Langsdorffi, Trin.
Trisetum subspicatum, Beauv.

EQUISETACEÆ.

Equisetum (undetermined).

FILICES.

* Aspidium spinulosum, Swartz.
* Phegopteris Dryopteris, Fee.

LYCOPODIACEÆ.

* Lycopodium annotinum, L.
* Lycopodium clavatum, L.
* Lycopodium complanatum, L.

MUSCI.

* Hypnum Schreberi.
* Hypnum Castrensis.
* Polytrichum juniperinum.

LICHENES.

Cladonia rangiferina.
Parmelia (undetermined).

METEOROLOGIC

Date.	Time.	Locality.
1891. Aug. 4	8 A.M.	Rabbit Island, . . .
		Mouth of Grand River,
5	8 A.M.	Muskrat Island, . . .
6	8 A.M.	Top of Portage Muskra
7	8 A.M.	Top of Portage Muskra
7	9 A.M.	River level above Musk
8	8 A.M.	Sandy Bank, ...
9	8 A.M.	Pinnett's River, ...
10	8 A.M.	Gull Island Lake, . . .
	6 P.M.	Head of Gull Island Ra
11	9'30 A.M.	Head of Gull Island Ra
		Bottom of Lower Horse
	6 P.M.	Top of Lower Horsesh
12	8'45 A.M.	Top of Lower Horsesh
	6 P.M	Lower Ninnipi Island,
13	8 A.M.	Lower Ninnipi Island,
	6 P.M.	Ninnipi Rapid, ...
14	8 A.M.	Ninnipi Rapid, ...
15	8 A.M.	12 miles above Ninnipi
		Slackwater, ...
	6 P.M.	Slackwater, ...
16	8 A.M.	Slackwater, ...
	1 P.M.	Cascade, ...
	6 P.M.	2 miles above Cascade,
17	8 A.M.	2 miles above Cascade,
	1 P.M.	7 miles above Cascade,
	6 P.M.	Crescent Lake, . . .
18	8 A.M.	Crescent Lake, ...
		5 miles above Crescent
	6 P.M.	Trout Point, ...
19	8 A.M.	Trout Point, ...
	5'45 P.M.	Mouni Rapids, ...
20	8 A.M.	Mouni Rapids, ...
	4 P.M.	Wanakopow Lake, . .
21	8 A.M.	Wanakopow Lake,
		13 miles from outlet of
	6 P M	18 miles from outlet of
22	9 A.M.	18 miles from outlet of
		3 miles above entrance
23	8 A.M.	3 miles above entrance
24	8 A.M.	3 miles above entrance
		8 miles above entrance
	5'45 P.M.	10 miles above entran
25	8 A.M.	10 miles above entran
	6 P.M.	21 miles above entran
26	8 A.M.	21 miles above entran
	6'15 P.M.	34 miles above entran
27	8 A.M.	34 miles above entran
	4 P.M.	Base of Big Hill, . .
28	8 A.M.	Base of Big Hill, . .
		Top of Big Hill, . . .
		Geoffrey Lake, . . .
29	8 A.M.	Geoffrey Lake. . . .
	5 P.M.	Base of Big Hill, . . .
30	8 A.M.	Base of Big Hill, . . .
		Top of Big Hill, . . .
31	8 A.M.	Geoffrey Lake, . . .
		Fourth Lake, ...
		Big Lake, ...
Sept. 1	8 A.M.	Big Lake, ...
		West end of Big Lake
	6'30 P.M.	10 miles northwest of
2	8 A.M.	10 miles northwest of
	4 P.M.	Top of Grand Falls, .
	5'30 P M.	Base of Grand Falls,
3	8 A.M.	Grand Falls, ...

METEOROLOG'

Date.	Time.	Loca
1891. Sept. 3	8 A.M.	Tableland above (
	6 P.M.	Hill 12 miles S. E.
4	8 A.M.	Hill 12 miles S. E.
	5 P.M.	Top of Big Hill,
	6 P.M.	Base of Big Hill,
5	8 A.M.	Base of Big Hill,
6	8 A.M.	Base of Big Hill,
	6 P.M.	2½ miles below Big
7	8 A.M.	2½ miles below Big
	10 A.M.	3 miles above Lak
8	8 A.M.	3 miles above Lak
	5 P.M.	Lower end Lake
9	8 A.M.	Lower end Lake
	9'30 A.M.	Head of Mouni R
	11'30 A.M.	Base of Mouni Ra
	3 P.M.	Head of Slackwa
	6 P.M.	9 miles above Nin
10	8 A.M.	9 miles above Nin
	10 A.M.	End of Slackwate
	11'45 A.M.	Base of Ninnipi R
	12'15 P.M.	Head of Horsesho
	12'50 P.M.	Base of Horsesho
	1'30 P M.	Head of Gull Isla
	5'30 P M.	Middle of Gull Is
11	8 A.M.	Middle of Gull Is
	5'10 P.M.	Muskrat Falls,
12	8 A.M.	Muskrat Falls,
		Top of Muskrat I
		Base of Muskrat
	2 P M.	Top of Portage M
	3 P.M.	Base of Portage M
	7 P.M.	20 miles below M
13	9 A.M.	20 miles below M
	1 P.M.	Mouth of Grand

Estimated distance of Grand Falls fro
Estimated height of tableland above :
Mean Minimum Temoerature during
Mean Maximum Temperature during
Minimum Temperature registered on
Maximum Temperature registered on

APPENDIX C.

METEOROLOGICAL NOTES, GRAND RIVER, LABRADOR, 1891.

Date.	Time.	LOCALITY.	Minimum Temperature for previous 12 hours.	Maximum Temperature for previous 12 hours.	Temperature at Starting Point.	Aneroid at Starting Point.	Temperature at later mediate Points.	Aneroid at Intermediate Points.	REMARKS.
1891.									
Aug. 4	8 A.M.	Rabbit Island,	50	64	55	30·10	—	—	
		Mouth of Grand River,	—	—	—	—	62	30·12	Rain.
5	8 A.M.	Muskrat Island,	40	57	52	30·15	—	—	
6	8 A.M.	Top of Portage Muskrat Falls,	42	54	52	29·85	—	—	
7	8 A.M.	Top of Portage Muskrat Falls,	55	70	53	29·75	—	—	Rain.
7	9 A.M.	River level above Muskrat Falls,	—	—	—	—	66	29·91	
8	8 A.M.	Sandy Bank,	43	66	55	30"	—	—	
9	8 A.M.	Pinnett's River,	31	57	54	30·05	—	—	
10	8 A.M.	Gull Island Lake,	41	64	56	29·97	—	—	
	6 P.M.	Head of Gull Island Rapids,	—	—	—	—	61	29·98	Occasional showers.
11	9·30 A.M.	Head of Gull Island Rapids,	50	62	65	29·80	—	—	
		Bottom of Lower Horseshoe Rapids,	—	—	—	—	80	29·70	
	6 P.M.	Top of Lower Horseshoe Rapids,	—	—	—	—	80	29·68	
12	8·45 A.M.	Top of Lower Horseshoe Rapids,	50	69	65	29·56	—	—	
	6 P.M.	Lower Ninnipi Island,	—	—	—	—	70	29·54	
13	8 A.M.	Lower Ninnipi Island,	46	72	68	29·74	—	—	
	6 P.M.	Ninnipi Rapid,	—	—	—	—	74	29·72	
14	8 A.M.	Ninnipi Rapid,	52	62	56	29·86	—	—	
15	8 A.M.	12 miles above Ninnipi Rapids,	29	57	60	30"	—	—	
		Slackwater,	—	—	—	—	66	29·95	
	6 P.M.	Slackwater,	—	—	—	—	65	29·94	
16	8 A.M.	Slackwater,	39	61	64	29·94	—	—	
	1 P.M.	Cascade,	—	—	—	—	60	29·97	Cloudy.
	6 P.M.	1 miles above Cascade,	—	—	—	—	64	29·82	
17	8 A.M.	2 miles above Cascade,	50	61	60	29·75	—	—	
	1 P.M.	7 miles above Cascade,	—	—	—	—	65	29·75	
	6 P.M.	Crescent Lake,	—	—	—	—	61	29·66	
18	8 A.M.	Crescent Lake,	44	60	57	23·70	—	—	
		5 miles above Crescent Lake,	—	—	—	—	54	29·62	
	6 P.M.	Trout Point,	—	—	—	—	57	29·58	
19	8 A.M.	Trout Point,	35	59	52	29·63	—	—	
	5·45 P.M.	Mouni Rapids,	—	—	—	—	48	29·60	
20	8 A.M.	Mouni Rapids,	30	49	48	29·58	—	—	
	4 P.M.	Wanakonow Lake,	—	—	—	—	54	29·44	Rain.
21	8 A.M.	Wanakopow Lake,	45	53	48	29·20	—	—	Rain.
		13 miles from outlet of Lake,	—	—	—	—	54	29·12	Rain.
	6 P.M.	18 miles from outlet of Lake,	—	—	—	—	59	29·35	Rain.
22	9 A.M.	18 miles from outlet of Lake,	47	60	57	29·60	—	—	
		3 miles above entrance to Lake,	—	—	—	—	64	29·60	In camp. 81° max. temp. reg. during day.
23	8 A.M.	3 miles above entrance to Lake,	49	63	—	—	—	—	
24	8 A.M.	3 miles above entrance to Lake,	36	60	48	29·95	—	—	
		8 miles above entrance to Lake,	—	—	—	—	62	29·95	
	5·45 P.M.	10 miles above entrance to Lake,	—	—	—	—	59	29·92	
25	8 A.M.	10 miles above entrance to Lake,	37	52	52	29·96	—	—	Rain.
	6 P.M.	21 miles above entrance to Lake,	—	—	—	—	56	29·86	Rain.
26	8 A.M.	21 miles above entrance to Lake,	49	61	59	29·75	—	—	
	6·15 P.M.	34 miles above entrance to Lake,	—	—	—	—	61	29·75	
27	8 A.M.	34 miles above entrance to Lake,	40	56	50	29·70	—	—	
	4 P.M.	Base of Big Hill,	—	—	—	—	60	29·61	
28	8 A.M.	Base of Big Hill,	46	39	60	29·68	—	—	
		Top of Big Hill,	—	—	—	—	56	28·95	
		Geoffrey Lake,	—	—	—	—	55	28·80	
29	8 A.M.	Geoffrey Lake,	46	62	—	—	—	—	Rain.
	5 P.M.	Base of Big Hill,	—	—	—	—	44	29·55	
30	8 A.M.	Base of Big Hill,	35	46	46	29·77	—	—	
		Top of Big Hill,	—	—	—	—	50	29·08	
31	8 A.M.	Geoffrey Lake,	31	55	55	28·85	—	—	
		Fourth Lake,	—	—	—	—	58	28·80	
		Big Lake,	—	—	—	—	53	28·78	
Sept. 1	8 A.M.	Big Lake,	41	59	58	28·72	—	—	
		West end of Big Lake,	—	—	—	—	68	28·70	
	6·30 P.M.	10 miles northwest of Big Lake,	—	—	—	—	70	28·60	
2	8 A.M.	10 miles northwest of Big Lake,	47	59	54	28·50	—	—	
		Top of Grand Falls,	—	—	—	—	67	28·58	
	5·30 P.M.	Base of Grand Falls,	—	—	—	—	62	28·92	
3	8 A.M.	Grand Falls,	53	62	56	28·58	—	—	Rain. Violent gale ev'g.

49

METEOROLOGICAL NOTES, GRAND RIVER, LABRADOR, 1891.—RETURN JOURNEY.

Date.	Time.	LOCALITY.	Minimum Temperature for Previous 12 Hours.	Maximum Temperature for Previous 12 Hours.	Temperature at Starting Point.	Aneroid at Starting Point.	Temperature at Intermediate Points.	Aneroid at Intermediate Points.	Estimated Distance from Grand Falls, in Miles.	Estimated Number of Feet below Level of Tableland.	REMARKS.
1891. Sept. 3	8 A.M.	Tableland above Grand Falls,	53	62	36	28·58	—	—	—	—	
	6 P.M.	Hill 12 miles S. E. of Grand Falls,	—	—	—	—	45	28·42	12	+ 153	+ 153 feet indicates elevation of camp *above* level of tableland.
4	8 A.M.	Hill 12 miles S. E. of Grand Falls,	43	55	50	28·38	—	—	—	—	Rain.
	3 P.M.	Top of Big Hill,	—	—	—	—	55	28·74	27	192	
	6 P.M.	Base of Big Hill,	—	—	—	—	60	29·45	28	867	In camp.
5	8 A.M.	Base of Big Hill,	45	54	—	—	—	—	28	867	
6	8 A.M.	Base of Big Hill,	30	55	48	29·82	—	—	28	867	
	6 P.M.	2½ miles below Big Hill,	—	—	—	—	57	29·92	52	960	
7	8 A.M.	2½ miles below Big Hill,	40	53	50	29·70	—	—	52	960	
	10 A.M.	3 miles above Lake Wanakopow	—	—	—	—	53	29·76	67	1,017	Rain.
8	8 A.M.	3 miles above Lake Wanakopow,	41	56	45	29·58	—	—	67	1,017	
	5 P.M.	Lower end Lake Wanakopow,	—	—	—	—	50	29·58	105	1,017	
9	8 A.M.	Lower end Lake Wanakopow,	33	47	41	29·42	—	—	105	1,017	
	9.30 A.M.	Head of Mouni Budds,	—	—	—	—	51	29·42	110	1,017	
	11.30 A.M.	Base of Mouni Rapids,	—	—	—	—	58	29·55	120	1,138	
	3 P.M.	Head of Slackwater,	—	—	—	—	54	29·61	130	1,192	Occasional showers.
	6 P.M.	9 miles above Nienipi Rapids,	—	—	—	—	48	29·64	145	1,219	
10	8 A.M.	9 miles above Nienipi Rapids,	38	50	44	29·85	—	—	145	1,219	
	10 A.M.	End of Slackwater,	—	—	—	—	47	29·90	150	1,262	
	11.45 A.M.	Base of Nienipi Rapids,	—	—	—	—	49	29·92	156	1,284	
	12.15 P.M.	Head of Horseshoe Rapids,	—	—	—	—	51	29·94	160	1,302	
	12.50 P.J.	Base of Horseshoe Rapids,	—	—	—	—	52	29·95	166	1,311	
	1.30 P.M.	Head of Gull Island Rapids,	—	—	—	—	55	29·95	169	1,311	
	5.30 P.M.	Middle of Gull Island Lake,	—	—	—	—	65	29·96	178	1,338	
11	8 A.M.	Middle of Gull Island Lake,	42	57	55	29·94	—	—	178	1,338	Occasional showers.
	5·10 P.M.	Muskrat Falls,	—	—	—	—	57	30·02	206	1,411	
12	8 A.M.	Muskrat Falls,	31	46	—	—	—	—	206	1,411	
		Top of Muskrat Falls,	—	—	—	—	71	29·95	206	1,411	
		Base of Muskrat Falls,	—	—	—	—	73	30·02	208	1,477	Height of Muskrat Falls, 66 ft.
	2 P.M.	Top of Portage Muskrat Falls,	—	—	—	—	77	29·85	208	—	
	3 P.M.	Base of Portage Muskrat Falls,	—	—	—	—	71	30·07	208	—	Height of portage, 210 feet.
	7 P.M.	20 miles below Muskrat Fall,	—	—	—	—	—	—	221	—	No perceptible drop in river below Muskrat Falls.
13	9 A.M.	20 miles below Muskrat Falls,	55	65	—	—	—	—	228	—	
	1 P.M.	Mouth of Grand River,	—	—	—	—	—	—	233	—	

Estimated distance of Grand Falls from mouth of Grand River, ... 233 miles.
Estimated height of tableland above sea level, ... 1,477 feet.
Mean Minimum Temperature during 41 nights of journey, ... = 42°
Mean Maximum Temperature during 41 nights of journey, ... = 5A°
Minimum Temperature registered on journey, ... August 15th = 29°
Maximum Temperature registered on journey, ... August 13th = 72°

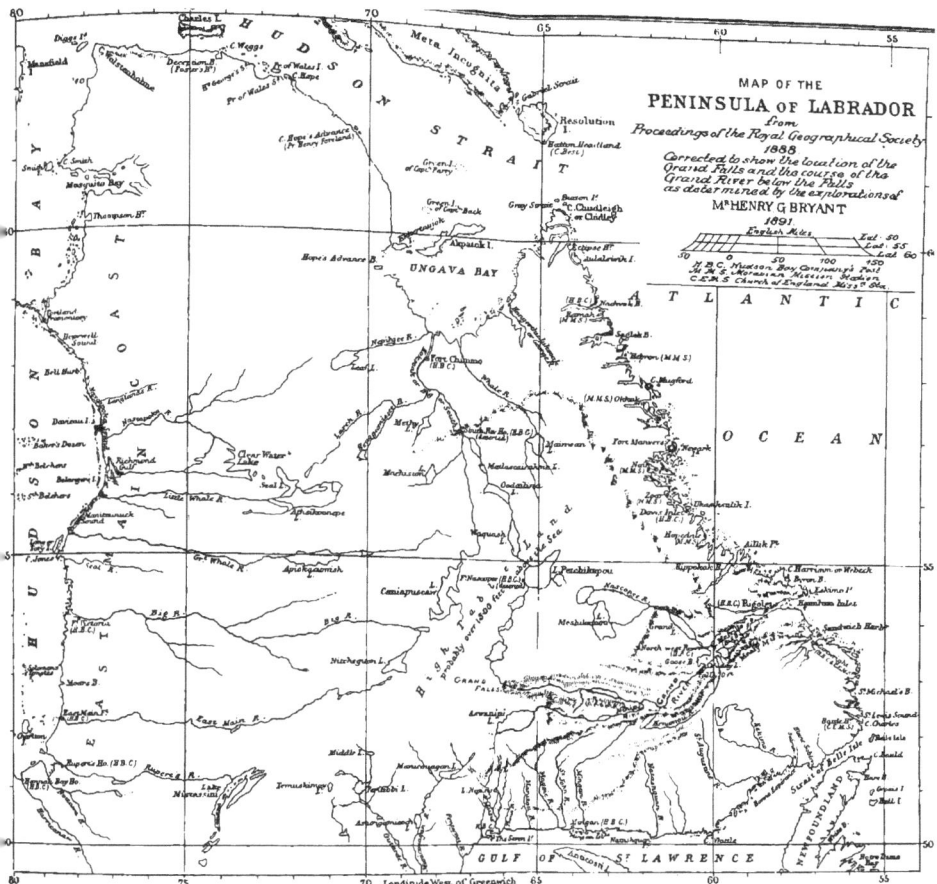

MAP OF THE
PENINSULA OF LABRADOR
from
Proceedings of the Royal Geographical Society
1888
Corrected to show the location of the
Grand Falls and the course of the
Grand River below the Falls
as determined by the explorations of
Mr HENRY G BRYANT
1891.

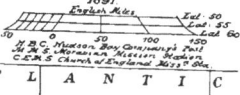

English Miles

H.B.C. Hudson Bay Company's Post
M & S Moravian Mission Station
C.E.M.S Church of England Miss.n Sta.

HUDSON STRAIT

Meta Incognita

Resolution I.

UNGAVA BAY

ATLANTIC OCEAN

HUDSON BAY

HUDSON COAST

Clear Water Lake

Grand Falls

GRAND FALLS

probably over 1500 feet

NEWFOUNDLAND

GULF OF ST LAWRENCE

Longitude West of Greenwich

APPENDIX C.   CONTINUED.

.CAL NOTES, GRAND RIVER, LABRADOR, 1891.—RETURN JOURNEY.

LITY.	Minimum Temperature for Previous 12 Hours.	Maximum Temperature for Previous 12 Hours.	Temperature at Starting Point.	Aneroid at Starting Point.	Temperature at Intermediate Points.	Aneroid at Intermediate Points.	Estimated Distance from Grand Falls, in Miles.	Estimated Number of Feet below Level of Tableland.	REMARKS.
;rand Falls, . . .	53	62	56	28'58	—		—	—	
of Grand Falls, .	—	—	—	—	45	28'42	12	+ 153	+ 153 feet indicates elevation of camp *above* level of tableland.
of Grand Falls, .	43	55	50	28'38	—		—	—	Rain.
. . . .	—	—	—	—	55	28'74	27	192	
. . . .	—	—	—	—	60	29'45	28	867	In camp.
. . . .	45	54	—	—	—	—	28	867	
. . . .	30	55	48	29'82	—	—	28	867	
; Hi'l, ...	—	—	—	—	57	29'92	52	960	
; Hill, ...	40	53	50	29'70	—	—	52	960	
e Wanakopow . .	—	—	—	—	53	29'76	67	1,017	Rain.
e Wanakopow, . .	41	56	45	29'58	—	—	67	1,017	
Vanakopow, . . .	—	—	—	—	50	29'58	105	1,017	
Vanakopow, . .	33	47	41	29 42	—	—	105	1,017	
ipids, ...	—	—	—	—	51	29'42	110	1,017	
pids, ...	—	—	—	—	58	29'55	120	1,138	
er, ...	—	—	—	—	54	29 61	130	1,192	Occasional showers.
nipi Rapids, . .	—	—	—	—	48	29'64	145	1,219	
nipi Rapids, . .	38	50	44	29'85	—	—	145	1,219	
r, ...	—	—	—	—	47	29 90	150	1,261	
apids, ...	—	—	—	—	49	29 92	156	1,284	
e Rapids, ...	—	—	—	—	51	29'94	160	1,302	
: Rapids, . . .	—	—	—	—	52	29'95	166	1,311	
nd Rapids, . . .	—	—	—	—	55	29'95	169	1,311	
aud Lake, . . .	—	—	—	—	65	29'98	178	1,338	
and Lake, . . .	42	57	55	29'94	—	—	178	1,338	Occasional showers.
. . . .	—	—	—	—	57	30'02	208	1,411	
. . . .	31	46	—	—	—	—	208	1,411	
'alls, ...	—	—	—	—	71	29'95	208	1,411	
?al's, ...	—	—	—	—	73	30'02	208	1,477	Height of Muskrat Falls, 66 ft.
uskrat Fal's, . .	—	—	—	—	77	29'85	208	—	
Iuskrat Falls, . .	—	—	—	—	71	30 07	208	—	Height of portage, 210 feet.
iskrat Fall, . .	—	—	—	—	—	—	225	—	No perceptible drop in river below Muskrat Falls.
iskrat Falls. . .	55	65	—	—	—	—	228	—	
River, ...	—	—	—	—	—	—	233	—	

m mouth of Grand River. . . . . 233 miles.
ea level, ... 1,477 feet.
41 nights of journey, ... = 42°
41 nights of journey, ... = 58°
journey, ... August 15th = 29°
journey, ... August 13th = 72°

www.ingramcontent.com/pod-product-compliance
Lightning Source LLC
Chambersburg PA
CBHW021512090426
42739CB00007B/572